Nests

Julie Haydon

Chapter 1

Building Nests

Some animals build homes called nests. Nests can be many shapes and sizes.

Many animals build their nests from **materials** that they find around them, such as grass and sticks.

a swan and her cygnets

honeybees

Some animals build nests from materials that they make inside their bodies, such as **wax**.

Chapter 2

Kinds of Nests

A nest can be a place to:
- lay eggs or give birth to babies
- care for babies
- stay safe from enemies
- keep food
- sleep
- seek **shelter** from bad weather

a mouse and her pups

The termites in this nest will spend most of their lives inside the nest. Other animals only build nests when they are going to lay eggs or have babies. Some animals make a different nest every night to sleep in!

a termite nest

5

Chapter 3

Ants

This hole is the **entrance** to an underground ant nest. A large group, or **colony**, of ants made the nest to live in. There are tunnels and small rooms inside the nest.

The queen ant lays eggs in the nest. The other female ants, called workers, look after the eggs and the young ants. Workers find food and take care of the nest, too.

worker ants

young ants

Chapter 4

Honeybees

Honeybees make nests called hives out of wax. They make the wax inside their bodies. Wild honeybees make their nests in places like trees and caves.

cells

The nests of honeybees are made up of **honeycombs**. Honeycombs are full of openings called **cells**. The queen bee lays eggs in some of the cells. Worker bees put honey and **pollen** in other cells. The bees eat the honey and pollen.

Chapter 5

Mice

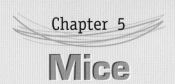

This mouse is making a nest in a field. The nest is shaped like a ball. The mouse **weaves** the nest out of grass. Sometimes it will make a nest inside an old bird's nest.

The baby mice are born in the nest. The nest keeps the babies warm and dry. The nest is off the ground. This helps to keep the mice safe from enemies.

Chapter 6

Swallows

This swallow has built a nest out of mud. When the mud dries, the nest is hard. The nest looks like a cup. Swallows use the same nest year after year.

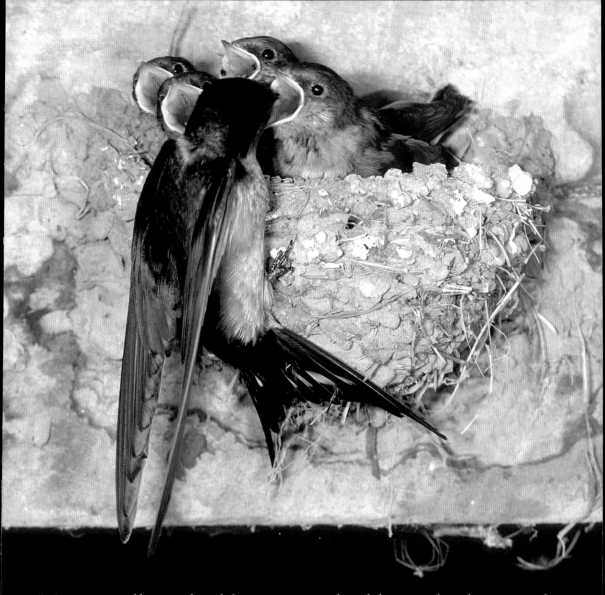

Many swallows build nests on buildings, bridges, and cliffs. They put grass and feathers in their nests to make them soft and warm. They lay their eggs in the nest.

Chapter 7

Eagles

These eagles have built a big nest in a tall tree. The nest is made of dead branches and sticks. The eagles put green leaves inside the nest.

The female eagle lays her eggs in the nest. The eagles take turns to sit on the eggs to keep them safe and warm. When the eggs **hatch**, the baby eagles live in the nest until they are old enough to fly and hunt on their own.

Chapter 8

Turtles

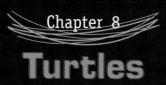

This turtle has dug a nest in the sand with her back flippers. She is laying her eggs in the nest. She will cover the eggs with sand to hide them and keep them warm.

The baby turtles hatch and climb out of the nest. They must run into the sea quickly. Many baby turtles are eaten by other animals before they reach the water.

Chapter 9

Crocodiles

This crocodile is making a nest in the riverbank. She digs a hole in the bank above the water, puts her eggs in the nest, then covers the eggs with dirt.

The crocodile stays near the nest to keep the eggs safe. When the babies are ready to hatch, they make noise. The crocodile hears them and digs them out of the nest. She carries the babies into the water in her mouth.

Chapter 10

Chimpanzees

This chimp is sitting in its sleeping nest. The nest is high up in a tree. Chimps build a new nest to sleep in every night.

This is how a chimp makes a nest. First the chimp bends over some branches. Then the chimp weaves the branches together. The chimp puts soft, green leaves in the nest to lie on.

A baby chimp sleeps in its mother's nest.

Chapter 11

More Nests

Do you know what these nests are made from?

Glossary

cells	small six-sided openings in a honeycomb
colony	a big group of animals that live and work together
entrance	the way in
hatch	to break out of an egg
honeycombs	structures made of wax inside the hives, or nests, of honeybees
materials	things made up of different substances
pollen	a yellow powder inside flowers
shelter	something that gives cover or protection from weather or danger
wax	a soft substance made inside honeybees that they use to build their honeycombs
weaves	threads fibers over and under each other to make something

Index